MEN'S EDITION

# THE SONGS OF
# BOUBLIL & SCHÖNBERG

21 SONGS FROM LES MISÉRABLES, MISS SAIGON, MARTIN GUERRE, THE PIRATE QUEEN, AND MARGUERITE

(with music by Michel Legrand)

ISBN 978-1-4234-4178-6

**ALAIN BOUBLIL MUSIC LTD.**

EXCLUSIVELY DISTRIBUTED BY

HAL•LEONARD®
CORPORATION

7777 W. BLUEMOUND RD. P.O. BOX 13819 MILWAUKEE, WI 53213

Dramatic Performance Rights controlled and licensed by
Cameron Mackintosh (Overseas) Ltd.
One Bedford Square, London WC1B 3RA England
Tel (171) 637-8866  Fax (171) 436-2683

Stock and Amateur Performance Rights are licensed by
Music Theater International, Inc.
545 Eighth Avenue, New York, New York 10018
Tel (212) 868-6668  Fax (212) 643-8465

Non-Dramatic and Concert Performance Rights are controlled by
Alain Boublil Music Ltd. and licensed by the American Society
of Composers, Authors and Publishers (ASCAP), One Lincoln
Plaza, New York, New York 10023
Tel (212) 595-3050  Fax (212)787-1381

Visit Hal Leonard Online at
**www.halleonard.com**

# CONTENTS BY SONG

| PAGE | TITLE | SHOW |
|------|-------|------|
| 4 | A LA VOLONTÉ DU PEUPLE (FRENCH VERSION OF "DO YOU HEAR THE PEOPLE SING?") | LES MISÉRABLES |
| 12 | THE AMERICAN DREAM | MISS SAIGON |
| 22 | BRING HIM HOME | LES MISÉRABLES |
| 26 | BUI-DOI | MISS SAIGON |
| 7 | DO YOU HEAR THE PEOPLE SING? | LES MISÉRABLES |
| 32 | DOG EATS DOG | LES MISÉRABLES |
| 42 | DRINK WITH ME (TO DAYS GONE BY) | LES MISÉRABLES |
| 46 | EMPTY CHAIRS AT EMPTY TABLES | LES MISÉRABLES |
| 37 | I WILL MAKE YOU PROUD | MARTIN GUERRE |
| 50 | I'LL BE THERE | THE PIRATE QUEEN |
| 61 | I'M MARTIN GUERRE | MARTIN GUERRE |
| 68 | IF YOU WANT TO DIE IN BED | MISS SAIGON |
| 78 | INTOXICATION | MARGUERITE |
| 82 | JAVERT'S SUICIDE | LES MISÉRABLES |
| 89 | LIVE WITH SOMEBODY YOU LOVE | MARTIN GUERRE |
| 96 | STARS | LES MISÉRABLES |
| 101 | SURRENDER | THE PIRATE QUEEN |
| 106 | WAITING | MARGUERITE |
| 109 | WHAT'S LEFT OF LOVE? | MARGUERITE |
| 114 | WHO AM I? | LES MISÉRABLES |
| 120 | WHY GOD WHY? | MISS SAIGON |

# CONTENTS BY SHOW

**PAGE**   **SHOW**

## LES MISÉRABLES

| | |
|---|---|
| 4 | A LA VOLONTÉ DU PEUPLE (FRENCH VERSION OF "DO YOU HEAR THE PEOPLE SING?") |
| 22 | BRING HIM HOME |
| 7 | DO YOU HEAR THE PEOPLE SING? |
| 32 | DOG EATS DOG |
| 42 | DRINK WITH ME (TO DAYS GONE BY) |
| 46 | EMPTY CHAIRS AT EMPTY TABLES |
| 82 | JAVERT'S SUICIDE |
| 96 | STARS |
| 114 | WHO AM I? |

## MISS SAIGON

| | |
|---|---|
| 12 | THE AMERICAN DREAM |
| 26 | BUI-DOI |
| 68 | IF YOU WANT TO DIE IN BED |
| 120 | WHY GOD WHY? |

## MARTIN GUERRE

| | |
|---|---|
| 37 | I WILL MAKE YOU PROUD |
| 61 | I'M MARTIN GUERRE |
| 89 | LIVE WITH SOMEBODY YOU LOVE |

## THE PIRATE QUEEN

| | |
|---|---|
| 50 | I'LL BE THERE |
| 101 | SURRENDER |

## MARGUERITE

| | |
|---|---|
| 78 | INTOXICATION |
| 106 | WAITING |
| 109 | WHAT'S LEFT OF LOVE? |

# A LA VOLONTÉ DU PEUPLE
## from *Les Misérables*

Music by CLAUDE-MICHEL SCHÖNBERG
Lyrics by ALAIN BOUBLIL

*Enjolras leads the ensemble, previously adapted as a solo.*

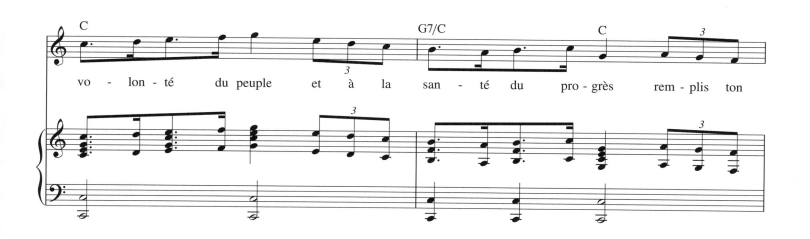

# DO YOU HEAR THE PEOPLE SING?

## from *Les Misérables*

Music by CLAUDE-MICHEL SCHÖNBERG
Lyrics by ALAIN BOUBLIL, JEAN-MARC NATEL
and HERBERT KRETZMER

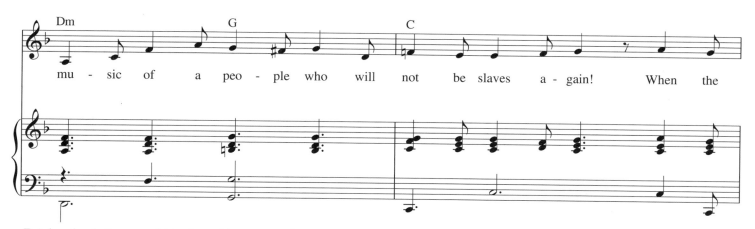

*Enjolras leads the ensemble, adapted here as a solo.*

# THE AMERICAN DREAM
## from *Miss Saigon*

Music by CLAUDE-MICHEL SCHÖNBERG
Lyrics by RICHARD MALTBY, JR. and ALAIN BOUBLIL
Adapted from original French Lyrics by ALAIN BOUBLIL

**Tempo di drag**

THE ENGINEER:

I'm fed up __ with small time hust-les. __ I'm too good __ to waste my tal-ent for greed. __

I need room __ to flex my mus-cles __ in an o-cean where the

big sharks __ feed. __ Make me Yan-kee, they're my fam-i-ly. They're sell-ing what peo-ple

*This song for The Engineer and Choir previously adapted as a solo.*

15

18

Wall Street is read-y to sell, the A-mer-i-can dream. Come make a life from thin air, the A-mer-i-can dream. Come and get more than your share, the A-mer-i-can dream.

21

# BRING HIM HOME

## from *Les Misérables*

Music by CLAUDE-MICHEL SCHÖNBERG
Lyrics by HERBERT KRETZMER and ALAIN BOUBLIL

# BUI-DOI
## from *Miss Saigon*

Music by CLAUDE-MICHEL SCHÖNBERG
Lyrics by RICHARD MALTBY, JR. and ALAIN BOUBLIL
Adapted from original French Lyrics by ALAIN BOUBLIL

*This song for John and Choir previously adapted as a solo.*

all the good we failed to do. That's why we know deep in our hearts that they are

all our __ chil-dren, too. These kids hit walls on ev-'ry

side. They don't be-long in an - y place. __ Their se-crets they can't

hide, it's print-ed _____ on their face.

# DOG EATS DOG
## from *Les Misérables*

Music by CLAUDE-MICHEL SCHÖNBERG
Lyrics by ALAIN BOUBLIL and HERBERT KRETZMER

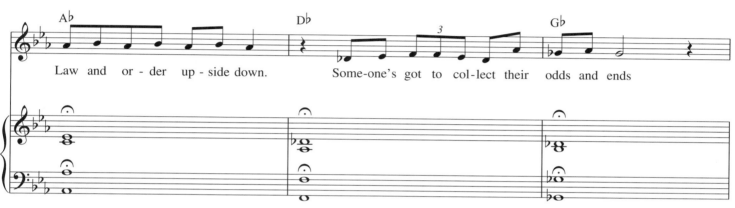

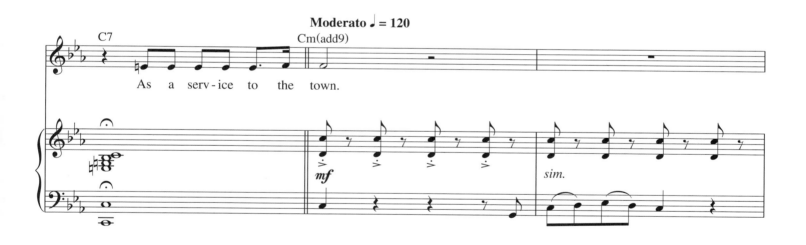

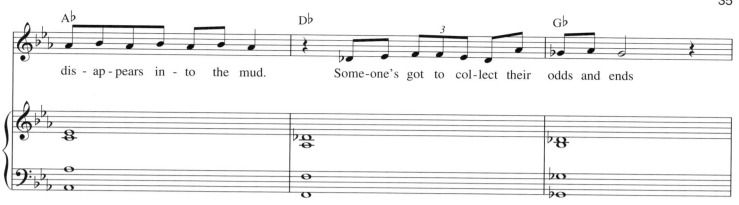

dis-ap-pears in-to the mud. Some-one's got to col-lect their odds and ends

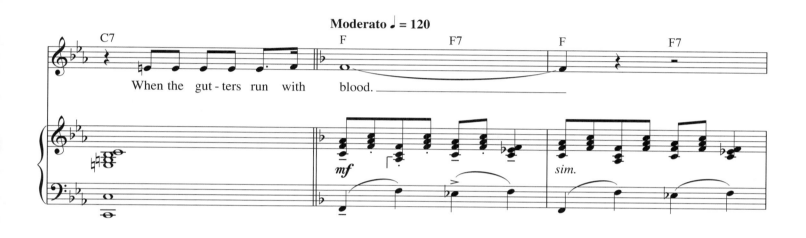

When the gut-ters run with blood.

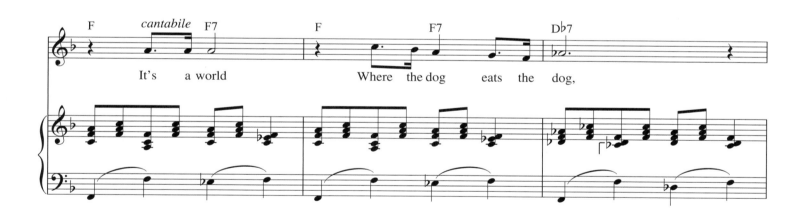

It's a world Where the dog eats the dog,

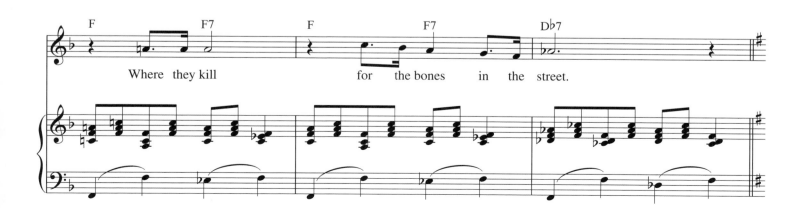

Where they kill for the bones in the street.

36

# I WILL MAKE YOU PROUD

## from *Martin Guerre*

Music by CLAUDE-MICHEL SCHÖNBERG
Lyrics by ALAIN BOUBLIL, EDWARD HARDY
and HERBERT KRETZMER

# DRINK WITH ME
## (To Days Gone By)
### from *Les Misérables*

Music by CLAUDE-MICHEL SCHÖNBERG
Lyrics by HERBERT KRETZMER and ALAIN BOUBLIL

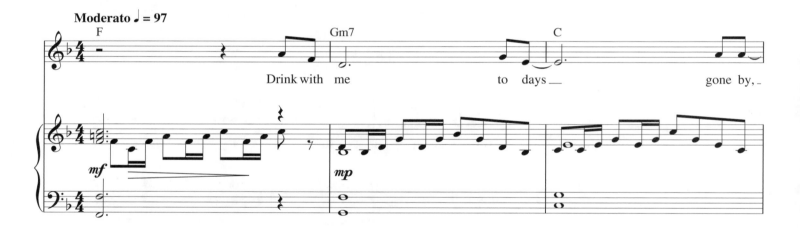

Drink with me to days gone by,

Sing with me the songs we knew.

*This song is sung by various student characters, previously adapted as a solo.*

Here's to pret - ty girls who went to our heads, Here's to

wit - ty girls who went to our beds. Here's to them and

here's to you! Drink with me to days _

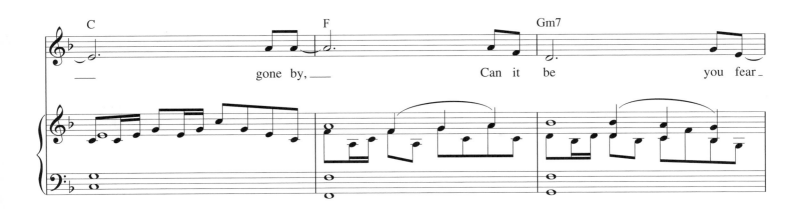

gone by, ___ Can it be you fear _

44

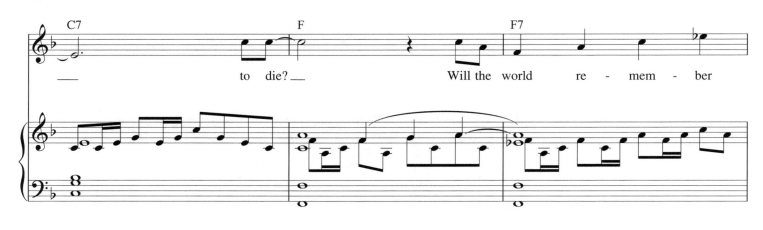

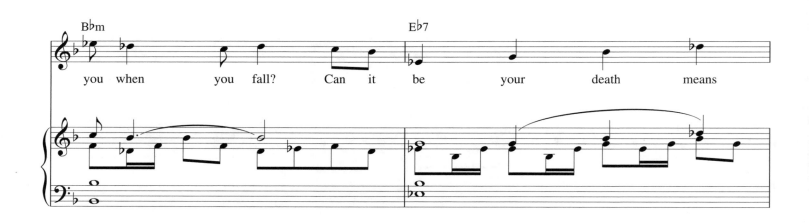

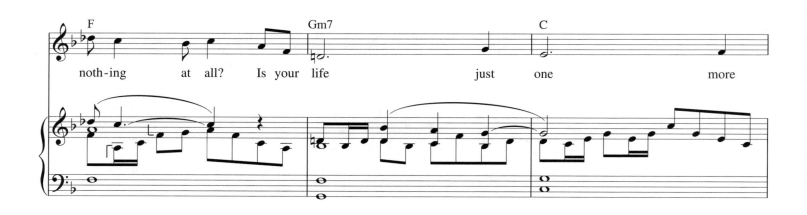

# EMPTY CHAIRS AT EMPTY TABLES
### from *Les Misérables*

Music by CLAUDE-MICHEL SCHÖNBERG
Lyrics by ALAIN BOUBLIL and HERBERT KRETZMER

47

# I'LL BE THERE
## from *The Pirate Queen*

Music by CLAUDE-MICHEL SCHÖNBERG
Lyrics by ALAIN BOUBLIL, RICHARD MALTBY, JR.
and JOHN DEMPSEY

bowed.

Go and mar-ry a man you don't love if that

pleas - es you.

Throw a - way, for a cause, all the joys we have

known.

I thought love's more than faith, more than clans, more than

an - y - thing.

May his kiss keep you warm, I'll be fine on my

# I'M MARTIN GUERRE

## from *Martin Guerre*

Music by CLAUDE-MICHEL SCHÖNBERG
Lyrics by ALAIN BOUBLIL and STEPHEN CLARK

62

Tempo 1

Guerre, fath-er I'm brave, and from your grave you'll keep me strong.

Yes, I'm Mar-tin Guerre, for they will learn when I re-turn that I be-

long. Soon_____ you__ will see_____ that

I can choose to__ be free. They all look for some-one to

# IF YOU WANT TO DIE IN BED
## from *Miss Saigon*

Music by CLAUDE-MICHEL SCHÖNBERG
Lyrics by RICHARD MALTBY, JR. and ALAIN BOUBLIL
Adapted from original French Lyrics by ALAIN BOUBLIL

chest.                                        Mean-while pack   a   sack, __

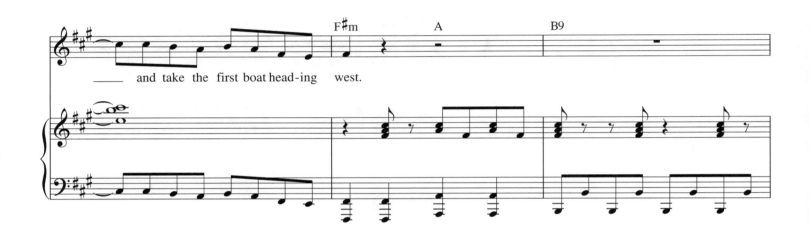

__ and take the first boat head-ing   west.

**Leggiero, meno mosso**

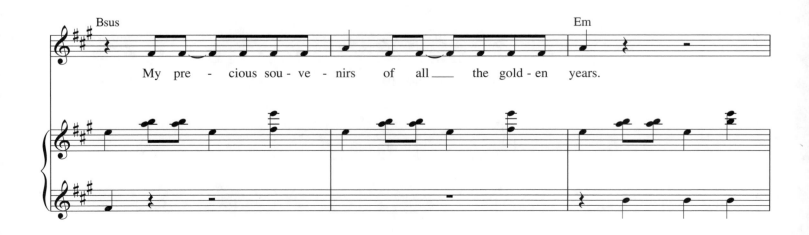

My  pre - cious sou - ve - nirs  of  all __  the  gold - en   years.

When your life hangs by a thread, don't cry __ a - bout the fates.

Grab a stash of cash __ and plan a rest-'rant in the States.

**Leggiero**

Let me stop for a bit. This was __ my great-est

76

# INTOXICATION
## from *Marguerite*

Music by MICHEL LEGRAND
Lyrics by ALAIN BOUBLIL and HERBERT KRETZMER

*This song for Armand, Marguerite and Otto previously adapted as a solo.*

# JAVERT'S SUICIDE
## from *Les Misérables*

Music by CLAUDE-MICHEL SCHÖNBERG
Lyrics by ALAIN BOUBLIL, JEAN-MARC NATEL
and HERBERT KRETZMER

84

85

I should have per-ished by his hand,                                    It was his

right.                    It was my right to die as well.          In-stead I live but live in

**Più mosso**

hell.                    And my thoughts __ fly a - part.

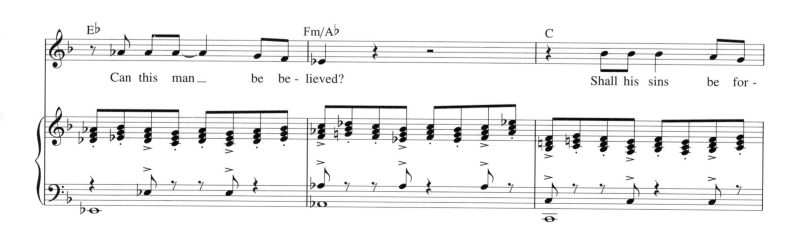

Can this man __ be be - lieved?          Shall his sins be for -

86

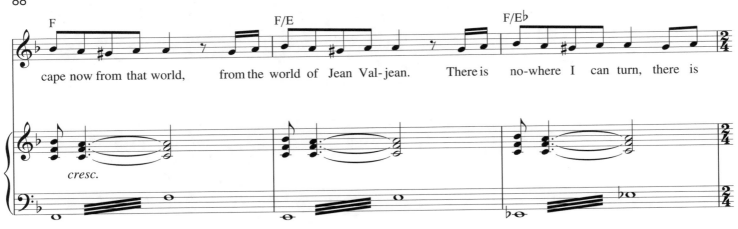

cape now from that world,  from the world of Jean Val-jean.  There is  no-where I  can turn, there is

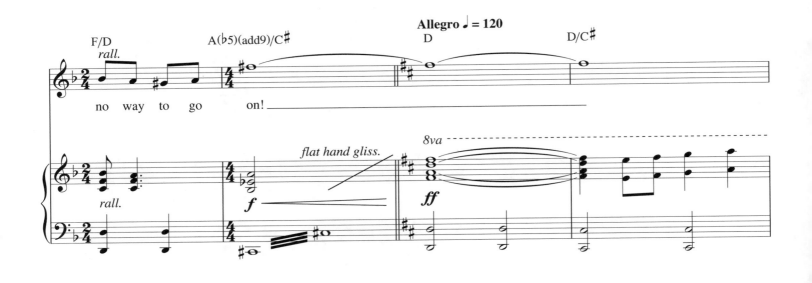

no  way  to  go  on! _____

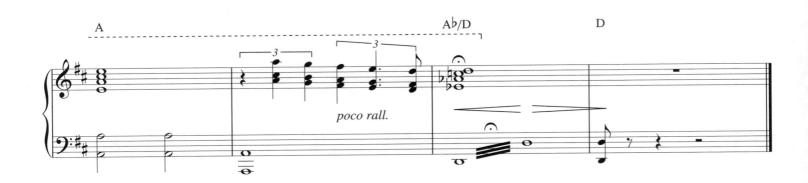

# LIVE WITH SOMEBODY YOU LOVE

## from *Martin Guerre*

Music by CLAUDE-MICHEL SCHÖNBERG
Lyrics by ALAIN BOUBLIL and STEPHEN CLARK

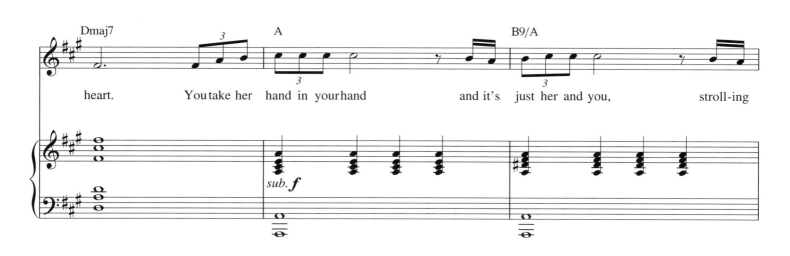

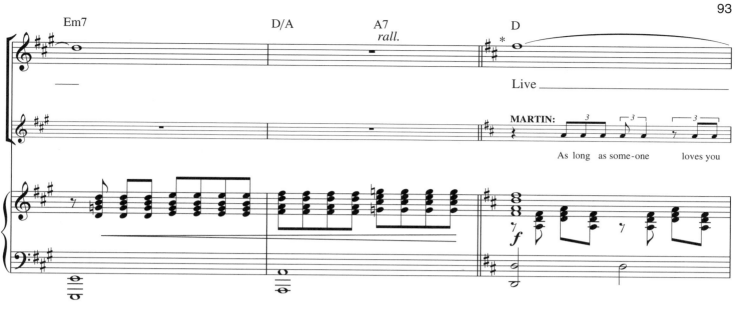

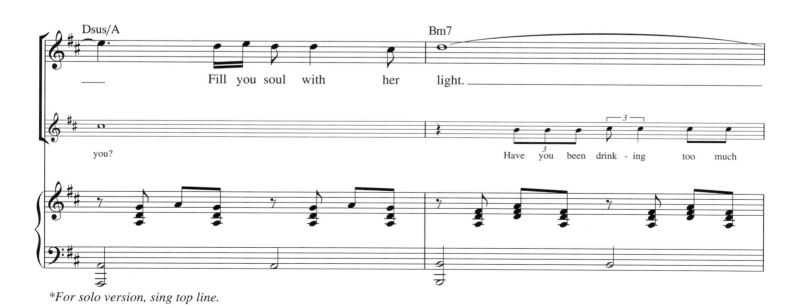

*For solo version, sing top line.*

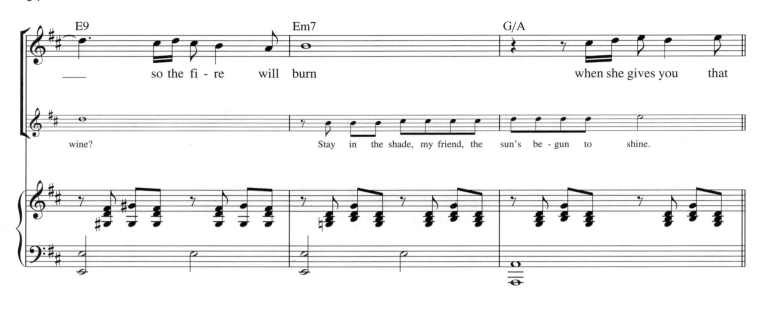

so the fi - re will burn / when she gives you that

wine? Stay in the shade, my friend, the sun's be - gun to shine.

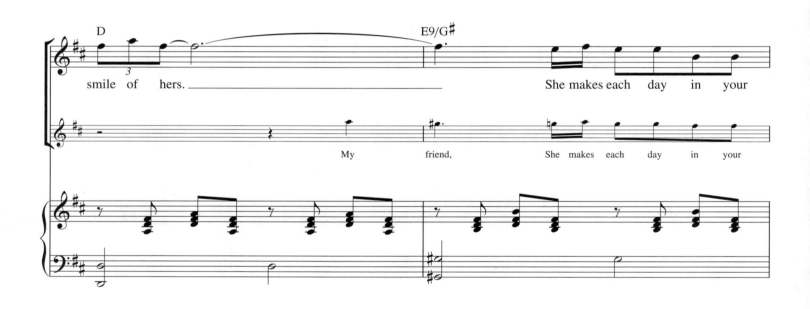

smile of hers. ___ She makes each day in your

My friend, She makes each day in your

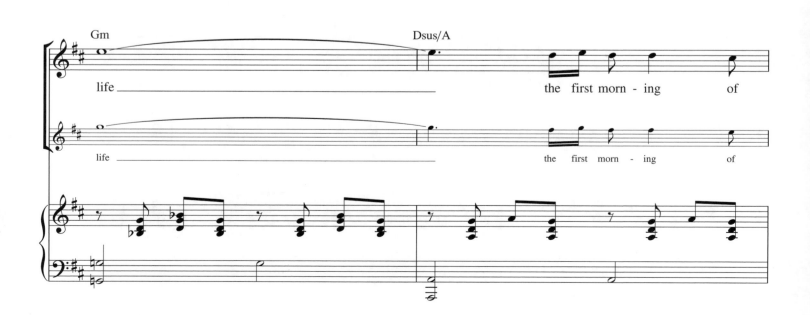

life ___ the first morn - ing of

life ___ the first morn - ing of

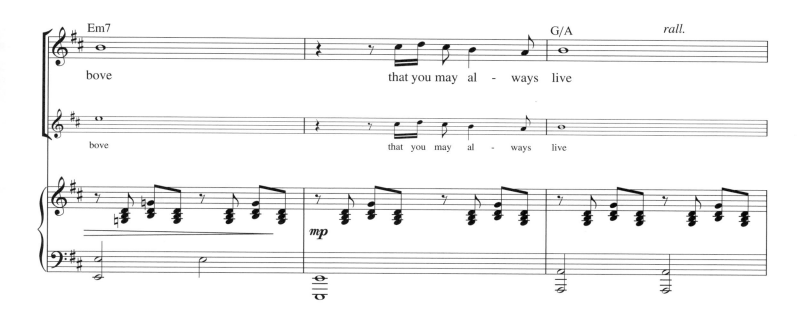

# STARS
## from *Les Misérables*

Music by CLAUDE-MICHEL SCHÖNBERG
Lyrics by HERBERT KRETZMER and ALAIN BOUBLIL

Page 98, sheet music

# SURRENDER
## from *The Pirate Queen*

Music by CLAUDE-MICHEL SCHÖNBERG
Lyrics by ALAIN BOUBLIL, RICHARD MALTBY JR.,
and JOHN DEMPSEY

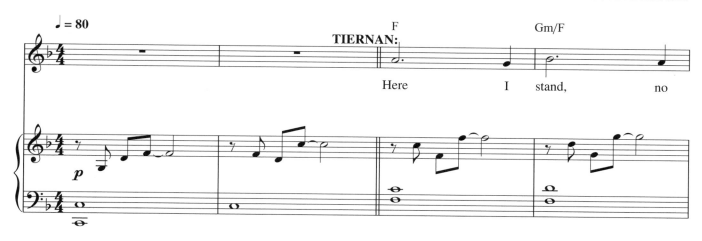

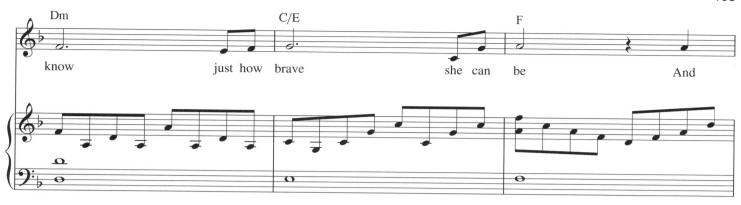

know just how brave she can be And

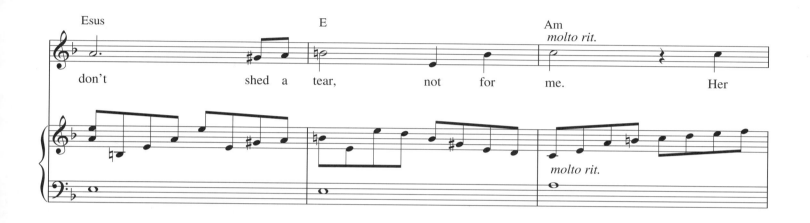

don't shed a tear, not for me. Her

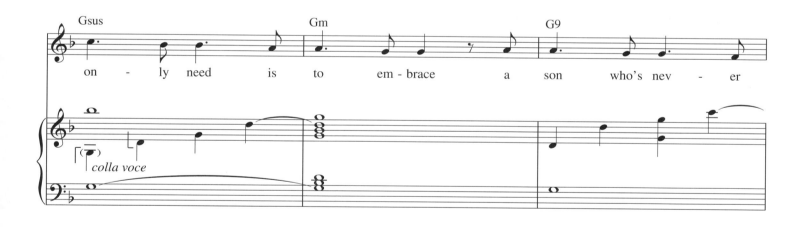

on - ly need is to em - brace a son who's nev - er

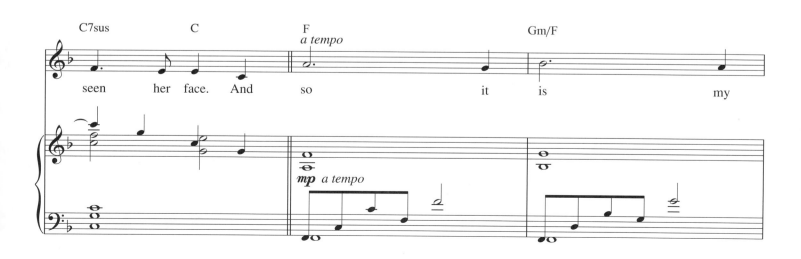

seen her face. And so it is my

set her free to heed her

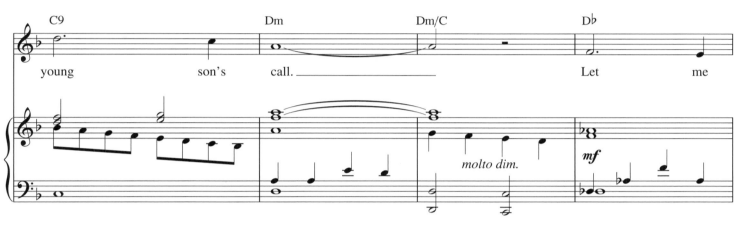

young son's call. _____ Let me

trade my life for hers And I'll sur -

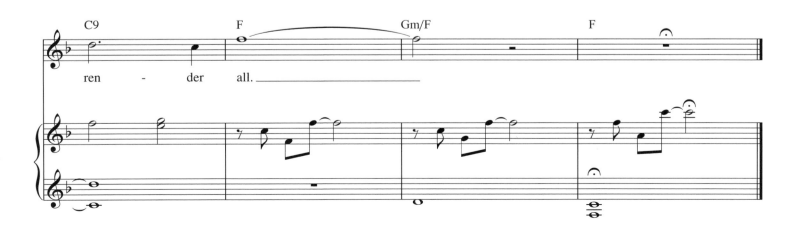

ren - der all. _____

# WAITING
## from *Marguerite*

Music by MICHEL LEGRAND
Lyrics by ALAIN BOUBLIL and HERBERT KRETZMER

*This duet for Armand and Marguerite previously adapted as a solo.*

# WHAT'S LEFT OF LOVE?
## from *Marguerite*

Music and Lyrics by MICHEL LEGRAND,
ALAIN BOUBLIL and HERBERT KRETZMER

113

# WHO AM I?
## from *Les Misérables*

Music by CLAUDE-MICHEL SCHÖNBERG
Lyrics by ALAIN BOUBLIL, JEAN-MARC NATEL
and HERBERT KRETZMER

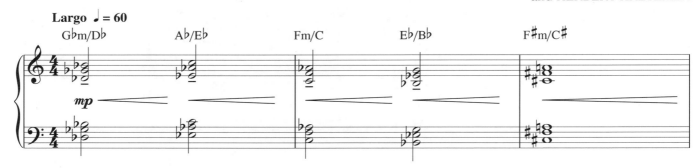

He thinks that man is me _ he knew him at a

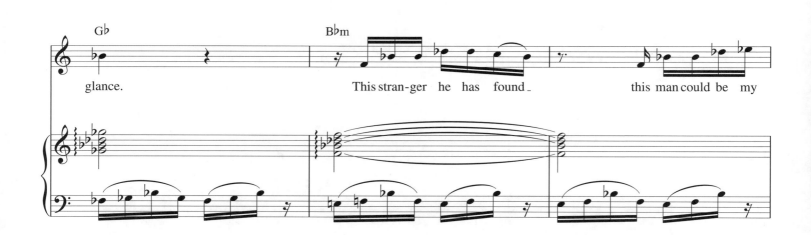

glance. This stran-ger he has found _ this man could be my

F♯
B
A6
I? I'm Jean Val - jean!
ff
G
B/F♯
D♯
rall.
D♯7/F×
And so, Ja - vert, you see it's true, That man bears
f
rall.
G♯m
G♯m/F♯
C♯/E♯
B/F♯
a tempo
no more guilt than you. Who am I?
ff
F♯
B
Two four six o one!

# WHY GOD WHY?
## from *Miss Saigon*

Music by CLAUDE-MICHEL SCHÖNBERG
Lyrics by RICHARD MALTBY, JR. and ALAIN BOUBLIL
Adapted from original French Lyrics by ALAIN BOUBLIL

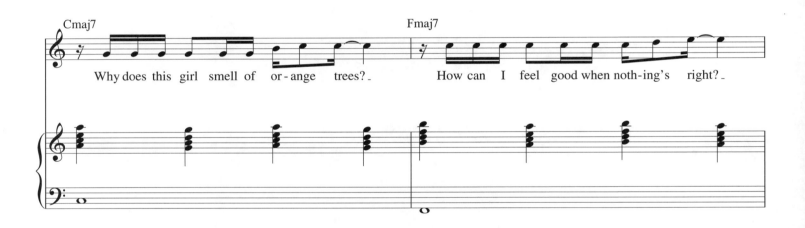

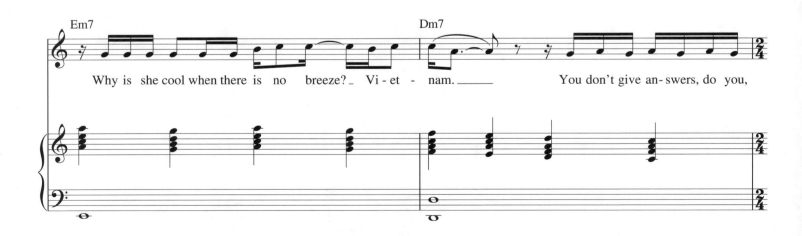

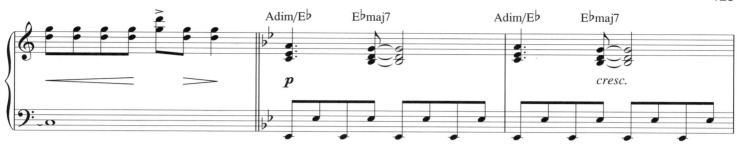

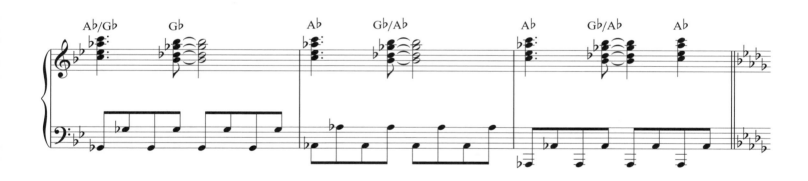

When I went home be-fore ___ no one talked of the war. ___ What they knew from T. V. ___